I Would Leave Me If I Could.

A Collection of Poetry

HALSEY

SIMON & SCHUSTER
NEW YORK   LONDON   TORONTO   SYDNEY   NEW DELHI

Simon & Schuster
1230 Avenue of the Americas
New York, NY 10020

First Simon & Schuster hardcover edition November 2020

SIMON & SCHUSTER and colophon are registered
trademarks of Simon & Schuster, Inc.

For information about special discounts for bulk purchases,
please contact Simon & Schuster Special Sales at
1-866-506-1949 or business@simonandschuster.com.

The Simon & Schuster Speakers Bureau can bring authors to your live event.
For more information or to book an event, contact the
Simon & Schuster Speakers Bureau at 1-866-248-3049 or
visit our website at www.simonspeakers.com.

Cover Artwork American Woman *by Ashley Frangipane*
Cover Layout Design by Garrett Hilliker
Interior Design by Ruth Lee-Mui

Manufactured in the United States of America

1   3   5   7   9   10   8   6   4   2

Library of Congress Cataloging-in-Publication Data
Names: Halsey, 1994- author.
Title: I would leave me if I could : a collection of poetry / Halsey.
Description: First Simon & Schuster hardcover edition.
| New York : Simon & Schuster, 2020.
Identifiers: LCCN 2020032873 (print) | LCCN 2020032874 (ebook) |
ISBN 9781982135607 (hardcover) | ISBN 9781982135614 (ebook)
Subjects: LCGFT: Poetry.
Classification: LCC PS3608.A54935 I18 2020 (print) | LCC PS3608.A54935
(ebook) | DDC 811/.6—dc23
LC record available at https://lccn.loc.gov/2020032873
LC ebook record available at https://lccn.loc.gov/2020032874

ISBN 978-1-9821-3560-7
ISBN 978-1-9821-3561-4 (ebook)

For my mother—

My favorite writing I've ever read will always be the pages of your journal I used to sneak into my room late at night. I only ever wanted to grow up and love with such a passion as you did.

For Professor Bradford—

I loved writing in your class so much that I dropped out to go love it intensely.

And for the fans—

My capacity to feel has been stretched and molded with each piece of your souls that you reveal to me. I offer this in return.

CONTENTS

INTRODUCTION

I've been looking for a place to put these pieces.

For 25 years I have flipped spastically
from FM to AM inside my head.
I am, still,
unaffected by the abrupt static punching through my ears.
I don't mind riding along to fragments and pieces
of the different stations.
I don't mind the indecision of a Motown record
spearheaded by a metal guitar solo.
The classical arpeggio climaxing
into the blue balls of worship music.
You know the sound, right?
An indecisive radio?
I have found a home here amongst the chaos.
The constant.

Every morning the muse puts her finger in my nose.
One, then two.
Sliding into me
pornographically.
She stretches my nostrils wide
until her slimy hand crawls past my deviated septum,
in between my eyes,
and into my brain.
Exploding into a fist
when she reaches the cavity behind my temples.

The muse is bratty.
She is smug.
She wiggles her fingers around defiantly.
She displays her palm expectantly,

waiting for a present I will drop into it.
She brushes and tickles the walls of my skull.
The muse is a flirt.
She'll always tease but never put out.
Fucking bitch.

I so badly want to be liked.
Scratch that.
I want to be loved.
I want her to love me.
Scratch that.
I want her to leave.
I want her to scratch that.
Scratch that itchy itch of my swollen brain.

It's only awful 'cause the muse looks just like me.
Dirty fingernails and gummy smile.
But she sparkles the way only a beautiful woman can.

A beautiful woman is a car crash.

Shiny asphalt and smoking rubber.
Melted plastic and metal edges.
Glimmering glass shrapnel iridescence
scattered across the road.
Haphazard beauty. Dignified and slightly terrifying.

The car radio flips from AM to FM.

The doors are locked and I'm trapped inside. My head bobs against
   the airbag.
It's calming. Like a mother's bosom. I would imagine, at least.
My mother was full-breasted. But loudmouthed, and sarcastic, and
   raised her babies out of our colic with camaraderie.

She didn't hold me close to the muffled beating of her heart
    beneath a department-store sweater.
She didn't breastfeed.

The nature and nurture in my sternum are arguing now.

My shoulders are held together by two rubber bands pulled tight in
    a schoolboy's hands.
Sometimes I feel like my spine will unfold and explode like a
    jack-in-the-box doll.
I can't carry all this weight, so I must put it somewhere and
    somewhere is with you.
You will take good care of it?

I want to walk away from my bones and set them down on a
    counter like my keys after work.
Let my skin sink into the armchair and lose its shape. Lose its
    form. Collapse into a sigh.

I see all things in this world as more beautiful than I, and I spin the
    details of their atoms in every paragraph and brushstroke.
I wish I had 11 hands with 55 fingers so I could paint and write
    and fuck and feed and grab grab grab everything.

I. Want. It. All.

It must be mine.

I want to walk away from the burgundy bags under my eyes and
    the periwinkle veins in my hands.

I hope you'll stay.

I hope you'll stay.

But I would leave me too, if I could.

DUE DATE

I was born 5 weeks early.
I couldn't wait
to join the rest of the world,
and that is
exactly
the moment
my enthusiasm ceased.
The nurses tried to take me so my
"mother could sleep."
But she refused to let me go.
I'm sure ultimately,
I ended up
in a common room for newborns.
And I'm sure ultimately,
I lay there comparing myself to the other babies.
Wondering if I were as smart as they were.
Or as funny.
Or as beautiful.
The average baby weighs 8 pounds.
I weighed 5.
The average baby is 20 inches long.
I was 14.
And it was on my first day on Earth
that I realized I didn't measure up,
and I never would.

I WANT TO BE A WRITER!

It is not a want.
It is not a wish.
It's simple.
A demon waiting
at the foot of your bed
to grab your ankles while you sleep.
It's a gnat burrowing into your ear
and laying eggs behind the socket of your eye.
It's sitting in your own filth for days,
staring at the shower across the room
while minutes become hours.
It's six months since you've talked to your dad,
And whining like an infant to your lover
begging to be spit-shined
like a piece of silverware,
"I have given so much to the page,
please tell me I am not worthless."

It is not a desire.
It is a clenched jaw and an aching back and a disposition to spite
    everything around you.
To find the world not worthy of your words,
and to find yourself unworthy of the world.
It is towering arrogance that says,
"Let these passages be free
in an existence that will cherish and worship them."
It is a terrible self-loathing
that sends your teeth sinking into your lips.

It's a gut pushed out
and shoulders slumped

and a sneaking suspicion
that everything you see is altered through your gaze.

They cry,
"But I WANT to be a writer!"
And my head hangs.

You are asking to be shot square in the head.
You know not what you seek.
You ask for bleeding brains
and carnage that stains your pillowcase.
You ask for jelly
in the place of the cartilage in your spine.
You ask for kindness that is never returned.
You wish to burn alive
in the flame of a love unrequited.

It's simple.
Write.

HOMEMAKER

listen to that
cool
cool
water run
never been good at being alone
say "hello holy father.
where's your daughter?
she could make this house a home."

you got a
new
new
closet
never been good at savin' cash.
chrome on the faucet
and you bossed it.
i've never seen you on the counter before.

listen to that
cold
cold
winter blow
never had time for absolutes.
new steam shower
for the powder.
his-and-her sinks
but
just
for
you.

you got a brand-new bedroom.
a clean set of sheets I've never seen.
thread count's pricey,
for your wifey.
i know she don't make the bed like me.
never seen a Persian rug look so homely
never heard a sadder voice
than when you phone me.
are you lonely?
you said it's time for some renovations.
time for conversation.
but I flipped houses
bigger than you before.

enjoy the silence
in your kitchen.
been watering all these plants
made of plastic
and you think they'll grow.

homemaker.
shiny new things but they're all for show.

SUMMER FRUIT

I spent springs and summers
as a child
eating the fruit from a watermelon.

Grainy sugar bites
and juice slick up my cheeks
like a Chelsea smile.

My mother used to warn me
if I swallowed a seed
it would get stuck in my belly
and grow a watermelon plant.
My stomach would expand
till I'd combust.
I always spit them out
in horror.

I spent a spring and summer
eating the fruit
from the flesh of your lips.
The bounty of two round mounds,
hard like pink sugar.
Your grip on my cheeks
with a firm hand
holding my mouth open.

To drop seeds into my belly.

To spit a virus in my throat
that grew into a giant "you" plant.
The branches
crawling up the walls of my insides
and begging
to claw my mouth open
and make me say things I don't mean.

The dying leaves
flaking off
and swaying to the pit of my stomach
in an imaginary breeze
landing with a deafening thump.

Echoes that bounce up between my teeth.

And remind my tongue there is no more watermelon.

Just empty space.

YOU WERE FIRST

So many men who came before you
So many women, one-night stands
I guess I found it easier
For me to charm a man
'Cause a woman always crumbled in my hands.

Could only act on what I knew.
Was raised to earn it that way too.
I guess I found it easier
to split men at the seams
At least that's what I learned in magazines.

All this
soft skin, soft eyes
All these
Beautiful laughs and beautiful thighs
Always kept me up at night
The truth is I was terrified.

Pink lips, warm curves
All these
Wonderful aching shaking nerves
Heart like it's about to burst
The truth is you were first.

I am angry because of my father.
Because he would come home
Wrinkled from work,
And slam the door so hard
the house would shiver.
I am angry because of my father.
Because his furrowed brow
Repeats itself in my Punnett square
And opens the curtains
On my forehead.
I am angry because of my father.
I can hold a grudge like it's a hand.
I throw my watch on my nightstand.
I am a worthless smudge
On the floor, in the rug
In the kingdom of the almighty
God who will judge
Me as hard as She can,
'Cause I won't love a man
Unless he is angry
Because of my father.

LAYERS

Thank you
for stumbling
across the universe
with your confident swagger
and tripping right into my lap.
Wild hair spilling across your eyelids
and nestling into my mouth
with my kiss on your forehead.
Thank you for the freckles on your nose
that keep me
star-crossed,
starry-eyed,
and then cross-eyed
when I'm lying underneath you
and I look up at your darling face.
You're made of everything good in this world.
Syrup-sweet and paining my teeth
dripping from my lips
like honey
from the bees buzzing in my head
driving me crazy, daily,
with the sounds of your voice
echoing through my skull
and the halls of my house
still ringing
from the last time you were here,
the last time it was a home.
Thank you for warming the industrial gray
of my concrete foundation
and turning my bones
from cement blocks
to rich mahogany wood.
Layers.

INVENTORY

He told me
about the women
he had slept with
when we were apart.
He was honest.
And I had asked for it.
He told me stories
decorated with leather
and violence
and anal.
Girls
who relaxed in sweet drunken smiles
and enveloped him in warmth.
Lazily tumbling
through bedsheets,
glowing in the acid hue
of the outside lights.
Girls
who wouldn't ask him
to pick up his dirty socks.
Or turn away from him
on a shared mattress.
Girls
who weren't sad and tired.
Girls
better than me.
Who had learned to turn their trauma
into adventures
for him to stumble blindly through.
Instead of wallowing
in their brokenness
and breaking everything
in their path
as penance.

BATTLES

Been biting my tongue till it bleeds
cry over things I don't need.
My mother told me
pick your battles wisely
but you made me angry
at the world
so I chose them all.

MEMORIZE

I'm a boyish
mess.
A boasting contest
with an inferiority
complex.
I can't make friends.
I've got an
eager desperation
to be up on
"what's next."
I have too much
sex.
I say it's 'cause
I'm anxious
and I'm
overly stressed.
I can't take blame.
I funnel through
liquor
and spit up my pain.
I'm no good
with fame.
There's a love/hate
relationship
with noise
in my brain.
Except
for when
you speak my name.
Because you take it in vain.
(Take it in vein!)
I could fall asleep

here.
Crawl inside
the sleeping bags
under your eyes.
But I stay
awake
to memorize.

STOCKHOLM SYNDROME PT. I

I remember
how the sky looked.
Your lips made my mouth numb.
Your face
grew closer to her neck.
It's easy to play dumb.

I remember
all the chaos.
The frantic, nervous sounds.
I don't remember much,
though,
once I hit the ground.

Everything went black.
Everything got cold.
I'm standing
on a sidewalk,
screaming,
"Over my dead body!"

I remember
tender spiderwebs.
All violet,
yellow,
blue.
It seems with one eye open,
still all I see is you.

I guess there was no casualty
that could make you refuse.
I hide
behind a strangled mind.
You tell me,
"Winners never lose."

A hostage situation.
I know I should,
but I can't leave
you
all alone
somewhere.
I know you don't,
but I still care.
This Stockholm syndrome
might just be the death of me.

I hope every single day you put your socks on backward
I hope you cry at night
and can't call me after
I don't hope that you'd die;
just live to 75
And you spend every waking moment
Wishing you felt alive.
I hope that some girl takes a picture
of your sleeping body.
Wish you could go a single week
and not hurt anybody.
I hope your coffee every morning
is bitter and cold.
I hope you're busy Christmas morning
and you miss the snow.
I hope your team loses the finals
I mean they already lost the finals
But the next one
And I hope that you scratch up all of your vinyls.
Hope you drive 80 miles
In your expensive car,
and run out of gas
in the wild.
I hope your knees ache
and your back hurts,
hope you lose your second phone
or can't remember the password.
I hope every girl unites and they decide you're a joke
But if they are anything like you
then I know that they won't
'Cause their self-esteem levels are fatally low.
So you bury your pain inside them

after the show.
I hope your brother turns out to be nothing like you.
Hope another year passes
and you hurt even more than I do.
Used to live up the street from you
but since then I moved.
My new house is clean
and the sky's always blue.
I sing in the shower
and I walk around naked.
I love my whole body
though you once made me hate it.
I eat lots of pancakes
and drown them in honey.
I've made lots of handshakes
and made lots of money.
I smile and sigh when I crawl into bed
'Cause there's no more scar tissue
inside my head.
I heard what you're up to
I'm glad that I left.
I feel like myself again deep in my chest.
Signed:
Sincerely,
Ashley

I wish you the best.

THE QUESTION

I stand before the mirror
and examine my breasts.
protruding forth from my chest
and demanding kindness, free
ice cream, and violence.
my speckled face, freckled pale
brown like organic eggs,
flushes pink.
my eyebrows unkempt
and short hair untidy at the crown.
I grip my buttocks.
dissatisfied.

I chase the paradox around my head.
The filmy, sticky grain of
femininity slides across my skin.
It twinkles in every stare
and as my weight shifts from hip
to hip, I'm gliding as I walk.
My clenched jaw,
my small lips,
my broad shoulders
like an adolescent boy.
I worship at the altar of
femininity in the women who
suckle the lavender from my breath.
It poses nothing to me
but a question
to which I do not have the answer.

I MET A MIND READER.

I have not seen the Sun in 7 days.
I have seen Frankfurt,
Oslo,
Copenhagen,
Reykjavík,
Helsinki.
5 countries
and 1 planet.
Just Earth.
No stars.
Just clouds.
And no Sun . . .

Earth is bleaker in the dark.
The gray hazy dark.
The upside-down and sleepless dark.
Not the romantic kind
that fills the gaps in between city lights
and candlelit dinners
and moonlight bouncing off of crystal glasses
filled with champagne, lipstick-stained.

I sat on an old bus,
packed in like crowded teeth in a young mouth,
and I saw a little girl.
She frowned at me.
I began to panic.
They say children can sense dread.
This is the first child who hasn't smiled
when I cast a glance in their direction.
Has my heart,
once so full of love,

finally drained itself like a yellow raisin?
Will the children begin to notice?
She looks at me quizzically and smiles.
Kicks her feet
and then shakes her head no.
As if to answer my question.
I met a mind reader. Aged 4 or 5.
I have seen light burst forth from a magic eye.
From a heart more wholesome than mine.
Astronomic miracles, in an unfathomable form.
But I still haven't seen the Sun.

THE TOURIST

I quite like how these jeans
Look hanging
'round your knees
And I love your dirty sneakers
When you kick them
off your feet

I'd really like to find
The place
between your eyes
Where I kiss you on the forehead
And make you smile
every time

I'm struggling to place
My favorite
freckled space
Between your hair,
hung
like a telephone wire
Swinging
'cross your face

And right now you're inside
My favorite studio
on Vine
Complaining
'bout a violin's
Misrepresented whine

And I can't wait to take you home
Where I can have you

all alone
And overanalyze each part of you
I've written
in my phone

See,
I've started taking down
All of my favorite
little sounds
That waltz around you
in 3 quarter notes
With each word you pronounce

It kills me that you'll leave
Off in a jet
over the sea
But I hope the air in California
Will forever
taste of me.

ONANISM

The corner of my childhood bed.
A stuffed bear, color: cherry red.
A toothbrush motorized inside.
A 15-mile dirt bike ride.
A pair of socks, balled up real tight.
A hot tub jet, alone at night.
Your kneecap, cased in denim jeans.
Victoria's Secret magazine.
16 years of bubble baths,
a showerhead that can detach.
A pointed toe,
a cramping calf.
Disgusted in the aftermath.

THE PARTY

Your tongue is in my mouth in the kitchen at the party.

Why the fuck am I at the party?

My dress is too tight for you to get your hands under,
but I left my panties at home tonight
and I'm dripping down my thighs.
My lipstick is smeared and there are people
probably staring
but fuck them anyway.
It's been a year and a half
of throwing glances in hallways,
and my hair standing on every end when you appear
and breathe down my neck
(so tell me, how the fuck I'm supposed to keep my cool)

So we leave for one night and it turns into five mornings.
Waking up and staying in bed for a couple extra hours
so I can see what color your eyes are
in that special light we only see at 6 a.m.
That silver peeking through the cracks
around your blackout shades
and bouncing off your brown eyes
that send me into a fully caffeinated rush.
Like they're soaked in coffee grinds
and I can see the steam rising off of their surface
when your gaze sets me on fire.

So we turn up the heat again.
And your sweat is dripping off your chest
and your open fist is around my neck
and I'm grinding into your lap,
rocking my hips against your weight
to match the ins and outs of your breathing.
(Can you tell that this is the pattern I'm following?
Your breathing quickens . . .)
Your teeth are in my skin
and you're pulling fibers of tissue from my lips and I wonder,

If I bleed, will you like the taste?

Now we're driving down the highway
and my head is in your lap.
Tasting the salt of your skin
and feeling you grow in my mouth
and the hum of the engine
is like a million fingertips between my legs.
There are people passing by in their cars unaware
and unassuming
but I'm praying they'll look over and watch me worship you.
Watch me work
to assure
that there is not a single millimeter of space in my mouth
that isn't filled.
Your hair falls out of place
and you clutch the wheel
and press your belt into my cheek.

I hope it leaves a mark.

And days later my tongue feels
like it doesn't fit in my mouth the same without you in it.

It's your laugh, and your calculating eyes.
Your wrinkled brows and the static in your grin
when you can't think of the right words to say
and I know it frustrates you
because words are the only thing
you've ever had total control over.
It's the feeling in my stomach
like the moment
you drop a scoop of ice cream
into a root beer float
and the entire thing threatens to bubble over.
Carbonated
and chaotic
in my chest.

It's the sheer comfort.
You're as vibrant as a stranger,
but as warm as a friend.
Like every day
I get reintroduced to someone I've known my whole life.
Like meeting myself in a mirror.
The way you take over my entire body
and mind

like you're putting your own personal filter over the lens of my life
so that I see it in your colors.
And my hands shake
and I swallow hard
when I realize how much nicer life looks in your saturation.
My brain buzzing
like the rattle of a neon light
at odd hours of the night
when I'm pacing
and wringing my hands,
counting the days till I see your face again.
And the irony in how fine life seemed before.
How quickly you made it seem like
nothing
would ever suffice
without you,
a part of it.

Why the fuck was I at the party?

THE BREAKUP

There is no combination of words in the English language,
that slice right between your teeth
with the perfect paradox of hate and love,
the same way as
"I love you,
like a brother."

THE PROFESSIONAL

I am currently seeking employment.
I am a professional holiday girlfriend.
I have great references
and highly impressive past work experiences.
I have been featured in 7 family holiday photos:
—6 Christmases
—and 1 Hanukkah.
Specialties include
my "famous brownies."
I will:
—do the dishes
—look through baby photos with your mother
—have a long list of baby names to suggest
for the child we will never have
but your grandmother will pitifully dream about us having
before she dies.
I have:
—plenty of clean, respectable dresses
—drinking games to impress your cousins.
World-class gift giver
and wrapper
(it's easier to nail it
when you only ever have to give one gift).
In one particularly extraordinary history,
I made a baby blanket from scratch
for a relative who was expecting.
I will never complain
about missing my family's festivities
for your own,
and I will accept contract termination by spring.
I am 5'4"
with a perfectly straight smile

(dental records included,
no history of braces)
and I will fill any empty space
in your family photo.
Please respond before autumn.

LULLABYE

sweet thing,
you hang like
a chain
around my neck
like a beesting
in August
in your hollow pain
I sweat
hollowed
we wed
I've gone cross-eyed
and tongue-tied
at the prospect
of your lips.
like a plaid-skirt-fitted virgin
with the devil on my hips
I'd melt like a mint
in the heat of your mouth.
like a hurricane in a dress shirt
headed angry
down south
I would give anything
to be slipping
down your throat.

VIRUS

I once had a fever so high,
I was left to my bed for 7 days.
There was a man,
Standing on my mattress with a shovel
Lifting chunks out of it angrily.
He wiped his brow and his sweat
Collected in the divots of my blanket
And made a little pond.
A scum pond,
With talking frogs and lily pads.
The pond grew deeper as the man dug harder and sweated.
I was drowning.
A goldfish swam up my throat and flopped around in my mouth.
I clenched my jaw and tossed and turned in the scum pond.
White and gray algae blinding me,
And filling my nose with fuzzy mold.
I tried to scream and retrieve the fish from the back of my mouth.
I was choking.
I tried to kick, but the man was standing on my legs.
His weight was too much to bear
And I feared that shovel would dismount onto my head
And split my skull if I provoked him any more.
I tried to yank the fish out again but it struggled.
It attached its jaws to the opening of my throat and it would not
    budge.
I yanked.
And I screamed.
And my mother came rushing into the room, tripping over her feet.

I was trying to rip out my tongue.

She fixed my blankets.

She stroked my hair that stuck to me like cotton candy dissolving in water.

I wanted to cry but feared I'd fill the pond again.

When my fever broke, I realized the man and the fish were all a dream,

And so was she.

LIKELY AS THE RAIN

I've always liked it
when it's sunny and warm.
You like it cold
'cause you're from the north.
Now I'm sitting by a window
watching rain fall down

. . . in California.

Looks like you always seem
to get what you want.
Even when it goes against
the natural odds.
'Cause it's 7 in the morning
and my bathroom's flooding
hard . . .

I never knew
what made you do what you do.
Tuck me into bed
and then you sneak off to
be somewhere with another
who's more like your mother
and doesn't expect as much of you.

An anomaly.
I'm not like you and you're not like me,
or how we used to be.

You know what they say,
the all-consuming rage
and unbearable shame,
of you losing me,
was as likely as the rain.

WATERMELON

He loves to bring me watermelon.
Spits in my mouth, seeds.
To grow inside my stomach like
A thing that begs to feed

I lick his lips from watermelon,
Spread across my cheeks.
And that pink sugar Chelsea smile
Is hiding underneath.

Now I devour watermelon,
Bouncing on his knee.
I rock my body back and forth,
So he can feel the heat.

I'm dripping like a watermelon,
Soaking through my seat.
I bite my lip and suckle on
The words between my teeth.

And oh the taste of watermelon,
Subtle but it's sweet.
I kneel down on the wooden floor
And beg him to proceed.

He fills my mouth with watermelon.
No one hears me scream.
To overdose on sugar is more
Painful than it seems.

My tummy hurts from watermelon.
He can be so mean.
But smiles like a gentleman
And licks my body clean.

And when there is no watermelon,
Only vicious weeds,
He puts his fingers in his mouth
To taste the way I bleed.

Now all I crave is watermelon,
Every time I leave.

BLUBBER

You went and caught a whale for me
Seven hundred days at sea
You cut him up in chunks
real neat
Turned him into kerosene

You said it was a present
You told me
to close my eyes
You tied me to a metal chair
And opened up
my thighs.

You rubbed me down in Vaseline
and pressed your body
up
against
me
You soaked me down
in gasoline
Lit me up
And then discarded me.

You said you'd always love me
from my
head
to my
toes
And then
All at once
you loved me to a little death.

PUSSY

Beautifully folded salmon sweater
Cashmere sleeves and slouching turtleneck
I want to slide inside
and feel the hairs on my arms
stand on end
Silver threads and white cotton
spilling from the seams
Japanese pink ginger
toffee and coffee taffy
Velveteen ear of a baby deer
Wrap around me like a ball python
swallow me whole
like a blind baby mouse
cinnamon in the swings
sour peach candy rings
Sweet surprise
She's open wide.
I follow like a moth to the bulb to fry.

THE MIRROR

I'm pulling
funny faces
in the mirror,
wiping down
the glass
so I see clearer.
I'm trying
to feel safe
inside.
My body
doesn't feel
like mine.
I look at who I am.
I think I fear her.

BAD DAY: I

I'm sorry
I'm having another bad day.
My bones are creaking
And my eyes leak
Like a broken faucet.

My mind is a bullet train
And I can't stop it.

I'm stuck in the middle of an avalanche and I'm not moving.

These things they come and go,
and I mean half of everything I tell you.
I'm half of everything I hate,
and half of anything I create
is you too.
So I start to hate the music when I hate you.

EIGHT

There was a mailman
I loved as a little girl.
He would stop at the communal mailbox
On the street
In the center of the apartment complex
And begin sorting mail away
Into 150 different little boxes
We lived in 1202
I would rush from my house
To greet the mailman
And he would talk to me as he worked
Filing away bills and cards and coupons
He would ask me questions
Quiz me
And give me a piece of Bazooka gum
For every question I got right
I would spin around and crush my sneakers
rocking up and down on my toes
I would curl one piece of hair
Around my finger while I thought of the answers
I would slide my tongue between my teeth
and the windows where they were missing
And between every mailbox
The mailman would look at me and smile
He'd pat me on the cheek
And tell me
That I was as smart as he was.
As smart as any man.
And I believed him.
Because why wouldn't I?
I was 8.
I knew that George Bush would win the election.

I knew the Pythagorean theorem.
I read 300 books from the public library
And I could draw every animal by memory.
I liked him 'cause he gave me chewing gum
And talked to me in his low voice
Calm and soft
Not the shrill, high-pitched voice
They would use on my baby brother.
One day the mailman didn't show up for work
I ran out and stopped in my tracks
There was a different man there
I asked if my friend was sick
The imposter ignored me
The new mailman showed up a few days in a row
The kids in the neighborhood said
The old one had a heart attack in a bowl of spaghetti
And died with noodles up his nose
I cried
One Wednesday I ran out to the new mailman
And asked if he had any gum
He told me to stay away
Because he didn't want to get in trouble like Charlie
I didn't know my friend's name was Charlie
And I didn't know how I could have gotten him in trouble
So I asked my mom
How you could give someone a heart attack
And she rubbed her head
and stretched her feet across the couch and said,
"It feels like you're gonna give me one right now."
I didn't want my mom to die too.
So I hid in my room
And I cried
Because I was 8
And a murderer.

IS THERE SOMEWHERE ELSE?

You arrive late.
Half-smile on your face.
Your tongue is thick,
I love the taste.
"Welcome to my new place."

Haven't seen you in a year,
you come out of your skin.
You're tripping on your sneakers,
beg I let you in.
I say,
"Where have you been?"
You answer,
"Where do I begin?"

You're coming early.
I mean this
figuratively.
Demeanor is cautious.
Unprovocative.
You're still
so fucking talkative.

"Haven't told you in a while,
but you're the reason for it all.
You're a vital complication
I never seem to resolve."
I say,
"Why all this silence?"
You answer,
"Mind's been so violent,
a tyrant."

You're boring me
with stories
of your unproductive glory.
You say the only thing
as good as that
was me.

I put you in my bed
again.
I take you down
like medicine.
Revisit the same old
regimen.
Just substitute
the gentleman.

WITH GREAT POWER COMES GREAT RESPONSIBILITY

I am not allowed to want to die anymore.
Believe me, I have tried.

TONGUE TWISTER

Peter Piper
picked
a peck
of people
he could utilize.
Built
a better
batch
of music they could advertise.
But Peter
never learned the way
that people compromise.
His only method to communicate
was to harmonize.
He never
ever
spoke a word
when we were feuding.
Major to minor
like the color of a mood ring.
I only liked him
when he'd play me something soothing.
Could understand him perfectly
if he did it while producing.
Emotions come and go,
they're either lovely
or abusing.
Maybe that's the reason
all my records are confusing.
We met in a studio and I couldn't break the silence
'cause he was raised
a Socialist

and I was raised on violence.
I had to be the best
and he was fine with trying.
Sometimes he built me up,
sometimes I was declining.
We got an apartment in a valley,
it was low enough.
Just like the song,
but we were far away from blowing up.
We fought like animals
and did the same when
making love.
I know that it seems crazy
but I really couldn't make it up.
The only time that it was easy was in transit.
I'm quiet in a car
'cause I was on another planet.
Felt like he didn't listen
and I couldn't understand it.
It was more than different languages.
I took it all for granted.
The summer killed me,
skin was crawling,
couldn't stay still.
A suicide
inside my body
(went onstage still).
I hear it echo
through the arena,
"Du er
et minne."

AMERICAN WOMAN

My insecurity
hurting me
all these boys gonna flirt with me
But my head down
on a mattress
famous actress
and she skrrrt'n me.
There's too much space
between her skirt
and
me.
"Let's take some tabs of acid
at Lake Placid,"
I say certainly.
Still too afraid to touch her
but it's
urgin' me.
She says, "You're staring
and quite frankly
shit is irking me."
I'm feeling hatred from the waitress as she's serving me
She thinks I'm spoiled
probably thinks I'm some suburban me.

Thinks I'm a child of a
Money-hungry
Prideful country
Grass is green
And is always sunny
Hands all bloody
Tastes like honey
But we're finding it hard to leave.

I got no space in my memory
Just some pics
of a friend and me
I got a mailbox
and a mansion
But no letters that you send to me
That house has haunted me for centuries
Should take a rock
and throw it at the windows
but they bend for me
I want to break some.
Ache some.
Feel like I'm awake some.
Meet with all my issues
And then
finally
handshake 'em.
And eventually when you tell me
all the reasons that you're leaving me
I have to hide them
so the people still believe in me.

THE FUNERAL

I finally killed my pride.
I saw you yesterday
and felt a funeral inside.
Like someone I love died,
and they asked if I wanted to see the body.

I know it won't be the same.
It will hurt me so badly
I'll choke on your name.
But how could I let this go?
I love you more than I love anybody.

This must be a nightmare
it couldn't be a dream.
I'll watch you in the shower
I'll rub all your limbs clean.
I'll rinse off all the wounds we caused
when we were being mean.
I'll dry you off and hold you
and kiss you in between.

Your friends will all be happy
and mine will wonder why.
Your mother will start to worry
why you made your lover cry.
My father will be angry
and you'll be left
alone.

HEREDITARY

I don't look much like my mother
But I know my kid
will look just like me.
With eyes that gleam
and razor teeth,
And Jordan 1s
on two little feet.
I'm impatient
and passive-aggressive
compulsive
obsessive
But mostly poetic
I'm whatever I've seen
on a movie screen
I grew up banging
on a pinball machine
I spent a lifetime
trying to wake up
and be mean.
But I will
never
believe
That I belong to the side
with the guillotine.
(You should eat the rich
Even if that includes me)
I still run
on gasoline
But my insides
are gooey
Like gelatine
I've got:

1. Cellophane in the place of a windowpane
2. A mixtape where I used to keep my brain
3. Daydreams running like an Amtrak train

I'm sunbathing in the door of an aeroplane.
Imagine if I weren't always busy all the time.
I would love to get a tan line
and call you from a landline
and maybe
hold
your
hand,
crash-land
In a land mine.

DRAMA QUEEN

Can you hear the silence of being alone?
The deafening stillness
of everything you've ever known?
Put on pause like a VHS tape
A full-on heartbreak
And you whine
and cry
and it echoes through the static of a television set.

Can you see the darkness of this void?
Bewildering emptiness of knowing that he had a choice?
Pause
like a checked cassette tape
An empty slate
And you scream and cry and it shakes
through the static of the radio waves.

Can you feel the fabric of being alone?
The rush against your skin
that vibrates all along your bones?
Pause like a broken zipper
A sterling silver whisper
And you shake and shiver from a velvet shimmer
(will you pull it down just a sliver?)

Loneliness never made for a good song
You've been singing on your own
all along
Writing records in your bedroom
since 15
Drama queen
Well you're older now it seems

Loneliness never made for a movie
No blockbuster Oscar, no silver screen beauty
Behind a Technicolor lens since 19
Drama queen
Well you're older now it seems
Why is everyone so mean?

TERTIARY

Peach clean
on a silver screen
He goes lime green
at the thought of me
He's got big dreams
like you can't believe
Been mean
since 23

Dark blue
like a deep lagoon
3 girls
in a hotel room
Missed calls
ringing to the tune
of dark tones
in your attitude

Soft gold
like a centerfold
He's got
no taste for the rock and roll
He's so
uptight and I'm no control
No reason to let it grow

Chartreuse like an aging bruise
He speaks
soft words but it's still abuse
I forget
when you sweet-seduce

We're in love
but it's no excuse

Tell me nothing changes when you leave me
But I been making changes, please believe me.

TELLTALE

I think it's for the best
if I should open up my chest
and mail the contents to your hotel room
to wake you while you rest.

BAD DAY: 2

I'm sorry
I'm having another bad day.
I'll yell and scream
and tell you things
like "I hate you."

My mind is the only place
where I can take you on.

I'm stuck in the middle of the ring, but I can't fight today.

These things they come and go
and I mean half of everything I tell you.
I'm half of everything I hate,
and half of anything I create
is you too.
So I start to hate the painting when I hate you.

TORNADO

I can feel it burn in my nose.
I can feel the tears swell
like raindrops in the corners of my eyes
until they get so fat
they threaten to slide down my face.
My fingers graze your arm
and I can feel little electric volts
wrapping up and around my wrists
like a spiral staircase
like a static handcuff
holding my hand hostage to your skin.
I can feel my heart climb into my throat
and curl up on the carpet
with its head between its knees,
to hide from the
beat
Beat
beating loud
like a thunderstorm outside.
I can taste the salt of your sweat
on the roof of my mouth.
I can remember the taste
like it's still on my lips
even when I am 3,000 miles away.
In my head,
I replay a mixtape of your laughter
sounding off from my phone
and I call you every 20 minutes.

I will hold your hand till my fingers are cold
and bluer than a Picasso
till the blood has left them.
I will kiss your head
and rub your shoulders
and bring you ease and ecstasy
till your foggy head stops ringing like a car alarm.
I will wipe every tear.
(I like everything about you,
even the things you give away.
Like tears
and laughs
and yawns
and lost eyelashes.)
I will be there when the sun comes up,
curled in your lap
shivering
rubbing my eyes and smiling softly.
I will listen to the same sad songs
over
and over
and over again
till they vibrate in my skull
when the volume ceases.
I love the sun for shining on your skin,
I love the wind for blowing through your hair,
I love the coffee for staining your teeth
and warming your palms in the morning.
I would protect you till the end of time.
I would lie down
in the middle of a tornado
and cover you.

LIGHTHOUSE

He was almost 7 feet tall,
with black oily hair
that stuck to his forehead in patches
like a Rorschach test when he'd sweat.
His bedroom was a dark, cavernous prison
at the bottom level of the house,
separate from the rest.
This granted him,
at first, privacy.
And, at the end, protection.
I used to love
being far away from everyone else in the house,
because it meant I could keep him to myself longer.
Keep him from being distracted.
But by the final days,
I cursed the distance
and would silently pray
that the earth would cave beneath us
and the bedroom addition
would grow closer to the main house
in a tangle of excavated tree roots and tectonic plates.
I silently prayed for an earthquake
so our guests could hear him scream.
He would stuff his nose with cocaine
for days on end
until the rims of his nostrils
were caked with white,
like cement,
and bleeding sores
leaking yellow-orange pus,
from him reopening the wounds
he had burnt into his airways.

He would pace the room in circles,
with his T-shirt sticking to him
in a cold sweat,
and cry.
A cry full of pain and loathing
that twisted his face
like pottery on an unmanned wheel.
He would punch himself in the head,
banging his fist
against his forehead
and temple
until his fingers
full of rings
left pictures on his skin,
and his knuckles burst open.
He would put his bleeding hand around my neck
and press me against the wall.
His eyes would flicker back to life
like a film projector malfunctioning
in a pitch-black cinema,
and before the title card ran,
he would stare
at the space between my eyebrows,
too cowardly to make eye contact,
and say,
"I'm going to fucking kill you."
And I would believe him.
So I would take his hand
off of my neck gently,
and wrap my arms around his head
like I was cradling a newborn
and stroke his hair
and whisper that it would be okay
and again
he would cry

that Siren's cry
like a warning to all ships at sea.
We'd resign into a damp bed,
and his knuckles would stick to the sheets
as the blood dried
and clotted
and scabbed
and I would lie awake as he slept
snoring through his coagulated nostrils.
I would stare at the ceiling,
too afraid to let a single tear escape
lest the subtle movement
be enough to wake him
from his docile state.
When he was sleeping,
he looked beautiful.
Like an old Hollywood star.
And with his eyes shut,
and the Siren scream no longer sounding off
from his slack mouth
in the master bedroom
detached from the home,
I became a lighthouse.
Dim glow beaming from my eyes,
a man in my arms,
kerosene running low in the tower.
Praying the gods would unleash their fury
and send waves so strong
they'd crash through the hills of California.
And the ground would collapse
and bury us both in the rubble.

THE PAINTER

My aunt had a tenant
who lived in a one-floor addition above her unit.
He had a fat red face and a heavy brow
and an accent that sent splinters underneath your fingernails.
He was a painter
who specialized in pointillism portraits of cherub boys
with Fuji-apple-red cheeks, dimples, and ivy leaves between their
    legs.
Hours of detail and perfectionism spent focusing his attention on
    every little inch of their baby skin and baby limbs.
My aunt hung one in her house that I would find myself
    staring at.
Half intrigued by his talent and other times to sit in the stillness
    of the stirring in my chest as if I were looking at something
    forbidden.
I dreamt about his studio often.
Sometimes the screen door would hang open and the smell of oil
    paints and turpentine and expensive ink pens would waft down
    the stairs.
On hot summer days I would lie in my tank top and shorts,
my tight curls tangling themselves like a frayed rug edge in a
    washing machine.
I would stretch across the carpet with cheap pastels and printer
    paper and draw girls.
Mostly faeries.
Naked and freckled with long straight flowing hair.
I drew what I wanted to be, and what was forbidden to me.
I wondered if all artists did the same.
I would lie there and the fragrance of his studio would travel
    beneath the door through the crack where the draft came
    through in the winter.
I was never allowed in the painter's studio.

It was a dream that was separated from me by a dark staircase that
    bled into oblivion like a nightmare where you couldn't move.
My eldest cousin strictly forbade me to enter the dark chasm.
I never saw him look the painter in the eye.
The staircase to the studio loomed like a stranger in a subway
    station.
It was a yawning fissure that I believed, if I could simply cross,
I would become a real artist too.
My family fought about the painter.
I would hide under the table in the spare room, while angry voices
    took the shape of shadows and bounced off the tile in the
    kitchen. I heard some strangers' names.
We didn't know much about the painter,
But we knew he had 3 children.
An older daughter named Rebecca who was born addicted to
    heroin, with longing coursing through veins that couldn't
    recognize what was absent from her new life. Too young to
    understand why she had an erratic aching wound in her heart.
We knew his other two children were about my age.
But they never came around.
One day I was playing in the yard alone.
Kicking pebbles with my Skechers and pacing between the broken
    basketball hoop and the fence that curtained my aunt's dead-
    end road from a used-car lot, he called to me from the roof.
He was working in vanilla-ice-cream-colored dickies, covered in
    haphazard smears of color, and holding 2 dirty glasses of sweet
    tea, and invited me upstairs.
So with the conviction of a child exploring terrain formerly
    unavailable to her,
I accepted the invitation and began the approach up the stairs.
This would be it.
I would burst through the door and run my fingertips across the
    glossy tubes of oil, and feel the brush hairs separate and fan out
    across my palm, and I would unlock the secrets to becoming a
    real artist. Like the painter.

But artists love what is forbidden to them, a fact I learned too
    young; too early.

I don't remember being in his studio.

It's an empty cartridge in my memory. I just remember walking
    down the stairs like I was holding a basketball between my legs
    in a relay race, and crawling back onto my aunt's carpet in the
    corner like a dying dog who didn't want to be seen.

Years later I was a 15-year-old on Christmas vacation when he
    came downstairs to our unit to make a plate of old ham and cold
    mashed potatoes.

My aunt was a kind woman who always offered her leftovers.

My eldest cousin sat in an armchair across the room and I watched
    his eyes follow the painter's journey to the microwave.

I saw the darkness of the staircase, and the emptiness of a memory
    erased in my cousin's eyes. The same foot planted, firm stare I
    gave the painter when his back was turned.

My cousin and I had many things in common.

The same furrowed brow, the same short temper, charming gummy
    smile, and aversion to touch.

And in all of these things I could finally see the difference
between what is the blood and what is learned.

I knew my cousin had walked the same stairs, he had smelled the
    oil and touched the brushes, and now we both sat on an antique
    carpet, cursing the same thing the painter stole from us.

I looked up at the wall, at the little naked child made of tiny tiny
    dots still held captive behind a glass frame on my aunt's wall,
and I wondered what the painter had stolen from that little boy too.

Flying above the quaint little houses under Heathrow.
London looks dirty,
but I keep this epiphany to myself in the baggage claim.
I land to a red-faced drunk at an outdoor pub.
He swaggers with unwavering confidence.
The brewing tension of a street fight.
Each step is like broken glass exploding on cobblestone that has
seen quarrels centuries old.
Slated in nostalgic hubris.
A nation birthed the oldest child.
It's too cold,
and too mean.
But poets,
they hate everything.
So I keep calm
And
FUCK OFF.

GUTS

I got this bad habit
where I don't think before I speak.
I fall in love like every week.
I keep a pistol when I sleep
inside my mouth
so I don't fight my tongue
for saying all these things,
like how I saw you in my dreams.
(I really did)
I'm getting bad at it.
So I just numb myself instead.
I'll cut my hair and dye it red,
and hope you get it through your head
that I'm in love
and it's bleeding through my skull,
but I've been hurt before
so I can't tell you
that I
keep this image
in my mind
of you sleeping
late at night.
I count the lashes
on your eyes,
keep my legs
between your thighs.
I could never tell you,
even though I'd like to.

I swear this never happens.
You know I've got a way with words.
I'd put a million in a verse,

but still can't bring myself
to face what I feel.
I'm scared of something real.
I should spit it out
and maybe get the guts to tell you.

The Seattle Public Library

Broadview Branch
Visit us on the Web: www.spl.org

Checked Out Items 8/17/2021 14:18
XXXXXXXXX4504

Item Title	Due Date
0010103965397	8/31/2021
The hill we climb : an inaugural poem for the country	
0010104589378	8/31/2021
Yoke : my yoga of self-acceptance	
0010102097077	9/7/2021
I would leave me if I could. : a collection of poetry	

# of Items: 3

Renewals: 206-386-4190
TeleCirc: 206-386-9015 / 24 hours a day
Online: myaccount.spl.org

Pay your fines/fees online at pay.spl.org

LAUNDROMAT

My mother would round up my brother and me,
Laundry baskets on her hips,
Like the *National Geographic* portrait of a mother
Carrying water
And her babies
We would march foot by foot
in the scorching heat
to the Laundromat
At the bottom of the hill
Of the apartment cul-de-sac.
The hill was massive.
It would be slick with ice and snow in the winter
And the big kids would sled down it
On homemade toboggans
Made of cardboard boxes
And laundry baskets.
Little rocket ships
For the poor kids.
We'd dive to the bottom
and ricochet across the parking lot
where the hill opened up into lawless concrete and pavement.
The wind would slice our cheeks raw red like sushi.
And beautiful girls
with beautiful button noses
turned pink like peppermint candy
would cheer from the landing.
In the summer the hill wasn't so charming.
My little brother is dragging his sneakers across the curb
nasty little thumbsucker
He used a pacifier till he was 5
And even as he slept,

his mouth would pucker and suck on nothing
Oedipus baby. Mama's boy.
I spit mine out the first time someone tried to put it in my mouth
I wouldn't be silenced
Infanticide!
We are marching
To the Laundromat.
We arrive and immediately
I run to a familiar friend.
A big black cracked leather couch
with yellow stuffing seeping from duct-taped holes.
It looks like a giant monster
in the dark corner under the decaying lights.
I stick my arm inside
And fear large teeth will bite it off at the elbow.
I imagine myself pulling out my arm
and it bleeding like a stick of salami.
The first time I ever saw a whole lot of blood
was when my babysitter Jessie
invited her friends over to my house
while my mother was at work.
She told me to shut my trap
and she'd let me watch any movie I wanted on TV.
I picked *The Shawshank Redemption*.
They sat outside the apartment complex
and 3 boys arrived and smoked cigarettes on the porch
One girl came inside.
She was bleeding between the legs.
Dripping in thick strips like the syrup
I used to make strawberry milk
She asked to borrow a pair of pants
I was half her size
I pictured her bleeding legs
and imagined my arm dripping with the same crimson.

I waved my pretend amputated stub around
screaming for my mother.
She didn't turn around.
She threw our still-damp clothes in the basket
And we marched back up the hill.

THUMBELINA

I am so thankful that your mouthful of 88 piano keys
charmed itself into my ear.
I am so lucky to have a handful of chocolate brown hair
in a bushel,
bunched up,
brushing my fingertips when you lie in my lap.
Your mouth slack and your pink lips parted ever so slightly.
Your rose-colored cheeks
and green eyes
and tan nose
and chestnut freckles
and blue-violet veins beneath the skin;
all the good colors of some angel
in a Renaissance painting.
Your eyelashes so soft and long
I close my eyes
and imagine them
brushing up and down the length of my body.

If only I could be so small
to lie in your eyelashes
as a hammock.
Swim in the whites of your eyes.
Dive off the Cupid's bow of your lip.
Hang with two hands
from the corner of your smile
like Peter Pan from a clock tower.
Dance and splash
in the tiny brown puddles
of every single freckle.
Crawl into the lobe of your ear
and hide in the seashell cavern
where I can hear the ocean
and whisper it back to you.

Your face brings me all the joy of the entire world,
right to my bed.
Right to my hands.
Right in the breath like a tide in your chest.

STUDIO CITY

I can't tell how to condense my life into 100 words
For a piece of paper
For someone to hold and have and abandon.
Really does a number on your identity.
It's not hard. It just hurts.
Because it bursts out of me like hot lava.
I find a million dandelions blowing through my head
and they are beautiful
But when they come at you like one furious wave
(a few times a day)
They stick in your nose and eyes and ears
You explode from the inside out
Like a time lapse of a decaying animal.
I don't want to walk around department stores
that smell like wax crayons
too bright
so everybody looks like a cartoon
Bleeding colors
And breaking the fourth wall
and I fucking hate parallel parking
the silence of Hollywood is deafening
and I will die if I keep eating every meal purchased from the store.
I feel like I'm made of plastic
I breathe and it doesn't reach my lungs
I eat and I don't taste
I cry and there's no burn in my nose anymore
I'm standing in the middle of a 4-way intersection
and a car is coming at me
and I have no idea which way to go.
Is this how it was supposed to feel?

EVERYTHING

Before I knew we were poor,

Everything

was magic.
An empty fridge
meant freezer-burnt Popsicles
for dinner.
Purple-blue mouths
and toothless smiles
calmed the torment
in my mother's crux.

Everything

was an adventure.
A shared bedroom
with my little brother
meant an eternal playmate.
A warm tent,
closed off by a blanket
hung from a bunk bed
and a hair dryer
snuck under the sheets to keep warm.
Arctic explorers
waiting for a rescue unit.

Everything

was a mystery.
Voices resounding from the living room
vehemently snaking

through the short halls
of the apartment.
And then one day,
I had

Everything

And

Everything

was over too soon.

TRAVIS

Travis was a junkie
All my friends were
I was a wallflower
I watched them tie up their arms and collapse onto couches
I was never high,
and always on the same strange slow ride with them
Travis rode a fixed-gear bike
He had nowhere to live
But never went without somewhere to sleep
Travis was handsome
He had a backpack and an iPad
And nowhere to take a shower
He would meet old ladies
Whose husbands had moved on or passed
He would make love to them
For a week or two at a time
Hold them in his arms
And stroke their thin hair
Kiss their lips, dissolving vermilion ridges.
He would paint their fingernails and take baths with essential oils
They would give him somewhere to stay and a few hundred dollars
And by Sunday, Travis would tuck a perfumed envelope into his
pocket
And ride off on his fixie
To score
And he would come meet us
With department-store lipstick on his collar
And a pocket full of sour candy and dope.
I asked him how he did it.
How it didn't rip his heart to shreds.
"I really do love them,"
he told me.
"All of them."

ANTAGONIST

Does a ghost
know that he's a ghost?
Does a saint
know that she's forgiven?
If no one knows,
then I don't know
if I might be
the villain.
I don't trust the author anymore.

BAD DAY: 3

I'm sorry
I'm having another bad day.
My tongue is twisted
my words come out
like venom.

I only use my armor when you frighten me.

Stuck in the middle of "I love you" and "I can't take this anymore."

These things they come and go
and I mean half of everything I tell you.
I'm half of everything I hate,
and half of anything I create
is you too.
So I start to hate the poems when I hate you.

THE BAKER

I baked him a cake,
and now I watched him cut it open.
The first slice always falls apart.
I winced, as the pieces crumbled like a landslide.
No matter how many cakes I bake,
the first piece that's cut
always falls apart.
The inside was cherry red.
Globular, bulbous chunks leaked from the center.
Like giant blood clots, bathing in buttercream.
I imagined I had taken my still-beating heart from my chest
and baked it into the middle.
He took a bite, and grinned at me.
His teeth stained like a row of garnets.
Now he could have it,
and eat it too.

ORDINARY BOYS

There are ordinary boys.
And then there are boys
who stick an arm down your throat
and grasp your heart.
Digging through your entrails
while your teeth rub
against the socket of their elbow.
You drool and it pools around your lips
and drips
to their armpits,
tickling down to their ribs.
There are boys
who you will write poetry for
as an offering
a gift
an insecure gesture, to say
"Please like me,
for I have gilded you in gold,
and therefore
you should love me
for the sheer fact
that I love you."
Then there are boys
who demand poetry.
Who keep you awake
at all hours of the night,
purging your brain
of their details.
Hoping
you can capture them on a page
and then capture them in the world.
You are choking

with his hand in your neck
and his fist around your heart.
Your aorta pulses.
And so does your aching pussy.
You write to calm the craving.
To corner them in fiction
And say
Finally,
I have conquered you.

FUN GIRL

I am the fun girl.
I am the spit hanging down from your tongue girl.
I'm the choke me as hard as you can girl.
I'm the give it all up for a man girl.
I'm the plaid skirt and white knee-high socks girl.
I'm a pistol that's loaded and cocked girl.
The don't mind when you call me a slut girl.
I'm the smack her real hard on the butt girl.
I'm a swallow my feelings and lie girl.
I'm a lie there and let him inside girl.
'Cause I don't wanna make him get mad girl.
I'm the better off being bad girl.
'Cause then nothing hurts when they leave, girl.
Except with his grip on your sleeve, girl.
You say yes to the threesomes and drinks girl.
'Cause you still really care what he thinks girl.
You're not boring or mean like his old girl
she was crazy, or that's what you're told, girl.
So you'll get further if you are the fun girl.
But you'll never be the only one girl.
You'll get older and wish you had known girl.
'Cause you gave way too much of your soul, girl.
Now you don't expect men to be kind girl.
You just use them and leave them behind girl.
It's so hard to grow up as the fun girl.
You'll be trapped in your days as a young girl.
A memory, for men you loved girl.
"Oh! That fun girl!"

POWERLESS

I'm locked in the bathroom on a
commercial flight.
Hilary Swank in a butch haircut
sends a hijacked plane
through my cerebellum.
I am sweating.
I pull my lips apart from my
teeth like a dental diagram
and I display my gums.
I sit to piss and roll my eyes.
cuff my jeans 2 times, 3 times.

I am in my memory.
riding a man on a mattress,
back arched like a prize horse.
grinding and grinding.
tossing my hair around
and gripping tight the ropes of ecstasy.
pornographic cries echo through
my head in the airplane bathroom.
they key-change, minor 5th to
humiliation.

I shift gears.
a woman beneath me, squirming like
a slug under a magnifying glass.
my veiny arms and slender fingers
graze across her like velvet.
why is the straight part of me
powerless?

LET'S HAVE BREAKFAST

The light is creeping past your curtains,
playing shadows on your head.
I wonder how much
I would have to beg
to stay till half past ten.
You won't notice
that I've overstayed my welcome
once again.
All great conversations
seem to
start in a
king-size bed.

DNA

My heart swings
in the balance
of this longing.
it is suspended here,
anxiously awaiting
sweet release.
tightly wound tension
throbs in my core.
swells
like an angry ocean.
rises
like warm bread
rich with yeast.
I tumble
weightlessly
through daydreams
of your skin.
the surface of which
bleeds
seamlessly
into visions
of your bottomless eyes
and the curve of your mouth

matching perfectly
the curve
of the small of my back.
I am spiraling
down a staircase
of lust
and comfort
and withdrawal.
I will lie back,
and slide through
the tunnel between
your double helix.
I will dive in your DNA.
I will stay here,
patiently,
comatose in the wake
of your everything-ness.
Your all.
I will make permanent residence
right here
in your acquaintance.

16 MISSED CALLS

It's another Monday morning
and you still haven't slept in your bed.
It's only been 3 days
but I'm told that
Jesus did a lot over the weekend
when we thought he was dead.

FOREVER . . . IS A LONG TIME

I spent a long time
watering a plant made out of plastic,
and I cursed the ground for growing green.

I spent a long time
substituting honest with sarcastic
and I cursed my tongue for being mean.

Weightless, breathless, restitute.
Motionless and absolute.
You cut me open,
sucked the poison
from an aging wound.

And now 50,000 war cadets
would cower at this small brunette.
To my surprise,
not 6 feet high,
who'd reach and grab the moon,
if I should ask, or just imply
that I wanted a bit more light,
so I could look inside his eyes,
and get the colors just right.

I spent a long time
calling all my parts by evil nicknames,
and I told myself they hate me too.

But you spent a long time,
tending to a home that's burning in flames
and your patience made me love you.

Build love, build god, build promises
build calluses, then build provinces
'cause I have found
somebody who would build life,
then demolish it.

And we could simply hit rewind,
to live it all a thousand times
find views in fucking Kathmandu,
to watch it from a different height
(and we'd comment how the sun shines)

I searched the world
to find
you hiding inside me
the whole damn time.

Weightless,
breathless,
restitute . . .

BAD DAY: EPILOGUE

"Swallow your apologies.
None of them mean shit to me.
And all you have these days
are bad days."

These things they come and go
and I mean half of everything I tell you.
I'm half of everything I hate,
and half of anything I create
is you too.

So I'll start to hate my future when I hate you.

L TRAIN

One day, just like any other day,
you will wake up
and something will stir in your belly.
It will shake
and growl
and rumble like a beast
and claw its way up your throat.
With two strong hands
it will wrench your lips apart
and force your mouth wide open
and you will say,
"I want it."
And you do.
Painfully so.
You will decide it's yours.
And from that moment forth
you will never be the same.
Your eyes will glaze
with a glimmering film
that lights up the dark
with its iridescent flickering.
Your teeth will grit and throb
and threaten to burst
like cracks in concrete.
Your stride will become faster,
stronger,
quicker.
Cutting through the air
like sharp shears through parchment.
Your pen will hit the paper
like a body hitting pavement
and you will scrape your knees red

over
and over
and over again
across the fine lines.
You will shut your eyes to the world
and retreat within yourself.
You will wait there.
Patiently.
Languid in the wake of your potential.
And then one day
You'll explode.
You'll shake your head
and laugh
and scream
with hysteria.
Every single eye
will focus on you
with laser-sharp precision.
You will have them in your grasp.
And your fingers
will fold
around them like shelter;
a dark ceiling closing in,
and you'll keep them there,
in your kingdom.
One day you will explode.
And your pieces will scatter
to far corners of the world
never to be found again.
You will trade these pieces
for that thing.
That thing you wanted.
You traded Everything
to have it.

HIGH-FIVE KIDS

Back to where it all began,
this time with another man.
'Cause mine has found his place
amongst the fountains.

One-hundred-dollar wine to drink
The blood pools in the kitchen sink,
and buildings line the windows
like the mountains.

Stuck in limbo,
I'm bent backwards.
Crooked spine,
and broken plaster.
Tell me, do you know the password?
We're denied by heaven's master.

Back to where
the pavement breaks.
Lined all along tectonic plates.
The stars soaked in the sidewalk
spell the message.

When all your lovers
start to die.
You wake alone
and wonder why
they left you here
to document the wreckage.

They tell me that it's art I make,
in all this chaos I create.

They tell me that it's much too late.
To rectify all my mistakes.

The kid is dead and gone
back to the
Kingdom.

HAVING

How strange to write about
"having"
when for so long
I've drawn inspiration only from
longing?

Pink cheeks.
Stubble ripples across them
like a flower
still clinging to the earth
it was plucked from.

Your eyes are static electricity.
You've missed me.

A STORY LIKE MINE

It's 2009
and I'm 14
and I'm crying.
Not really sure where I am,
but I'm holding the hand
of my best friend Sam
in the waiting room
of a Planned Parenthood.
The air is sterile and clean.
The walls are that
"not gray but green."
And the lights are so bright
they could burn a hole
through the seam
of my jeans.
My phone is buzzing
in the pocket.
My mom is asking me
if I remembered my keys
'cause she's closing the door
and she needs to lock it.
But I can't tell my mom
where I've gone.
I can't tell anyone at all.

You see,
my best friend Sam
was raped by a man
who we knew 'cause he worked
in the after-school program.
He held her down
with her textbooks beside her.

He covered her mouth
and then he came
inside
her.
So now I'm with Sam
at the place with a plan
waiting for the results
of a medical exam.
She's praying
she doesn't need an abortion.
She couldn't afford it.
Her parents would "like totally kill her."

It's 2002
and my family just moved.
The only people I know
are my mom's friend Sue
and her
son.
He's got a case
of Matchbox cars
and he says that he'll teach me
to play the guitar
if I just keep quiet.
The stairwell beside
Apartment 1245
will haunt me in my sleep
as long as I'm alive
and I'm too young to know
why it aches in my thighs
but I must lie.
I must lie.

It's 2012
and I'm dating a guy.

I sleep in his bed and
I just learned to drive.
He's older than me,
and he drinks whiskey neat.
He's paying for everything
(this adult thing is not cheap).
We've been fighting a lot.
Almost 10 times a week.
But he still wants to have sex
and I just want to sleep.
He says
I can't say no to him,
that this much
I owe to him.
He buys my dinners,
so I need to blow him.
He's taken to forcing me
down on my knees.
I'm confused
'cause he's hurting me
while he says "please."
And he's "only a man"
and these things he "just needs."
He's my boyfriend
so why am I filled with unease?

It's 2017
and I live like a queen.
And I've followed damn near
every one of my dreams.
I'm invincible!
and I'm so fucking naive.
I believe I'm protected
'cause I live on a screen.
Nobody would DARE

act that way around me.
I have earned my protection,
eternally clean.
Till a man who I trust
gets his hands
in my pants.
But I don't want none of that?
I just wanted to dance?
I wake up the next morning
like I'm in a trance.
And there's blood.
My blood.

Is that my blood?

Hold on a minute . . .
You see
I've worked every day
since I was 18.
I've toured everywhere
from Japan
to Mar-a-Lago,
I even went onstage
that night
in Chicago
when I was having a miscarriage.
I pied the piper!
I put on a diaper!
And sang out my spleen
to a roomful of teens.
What do you mean
this
happened
to
me?

(You can't put your hands on me?
You don't know what my body has been through.
I'm supposed to be
Safe
Now.
I've "earned it.")

The year is 2018
and I've realized
that nobody is safe
as long as she is alive
and every friend that I know
has a
story
like
mine.

(And the world tells us
that we should take it
as a compliment.)

But heroes like Ashley
and Simone and
Gabby,
McKayla and Gaga,
Rosario,
Ali.
Remind me
this is the beginning,
it's not the finale.
And that's why we are here,
and that's why we rally.

It's about Olympians
and a medical resident.

And not one
fucking
word
from the man
who is president.
It's about closed doors
secrets
and legs
in stilettos,
from Hollywood Hills
to the projects
and ghettos.

When babies are ripped
from the arms of teen mothers,
and child brides globally
cry under covers,
who don't have a voice
on the magazine covers
and you can't walk anywhere
if your legs aren't covered,
they tell us
"take cover."
But we are not
free
until all of us are
free.
So love your neighbor.
Please treat her kindly.
Ask her her story,
then shut up
and listen.
Black
Asian
poor

wealthy
Trans
Cis
Muslim
Christian
Listen.

LISTEN.

And then yell
at the top of your lungs.
Be a voice
for all those
who have prisoner tongues,
for the people
who had to grow up
way too young,
there is work to be done,
there are songs to be sung,
Lord knows there's a
war
to be
won.

STOCKHOLM SYNDROME PT. 2

Abandonment
is a complicated complex.
You're longing
for somebody who will leave.
I walked into a promised land.
A decorated,
perfect man.
With something vile
hiding up his sleeve.

I wonder
what I'll ever have control of.
Rejection breeds
obsession,
so they say.
I left my heart
and all my hope,
my vindicated tales of woe
in Sweden
on a freezing winter day.

LONG-DISTANCE RELATIONSHIP

that fleeting moment
at 4 a.m.
when I am shaken from a deep sleep
because I can't feel your skin
against mine.
when my entire body hangs
suspended
in that silver sliver of time
is a tiny speck of fear
that reminds me
that I love when you turn over
and kiss my neck

two feet of space
2,753 miles

any distance becomes too much to bear

a warm bed as wide as the world.

SMOKE

It's funny, the human fascination with smoke.
Every writer has flexed
and fucked
and abused the metaphor for centuries
"It vanished like smoke"
"Her body wound like a thin stream of smoke"
"I inhaled his presence like a cloud of smoke."
We are enamored.
Schrödinger's element.
It is there when we restrain ourselves from touching it,
And it disappears when we reach for it.
It looks solid, it holds form,
and then evades our grasp as if to taunt us.
Not transparent, not opaque.
Is it arrogance?
Smoke, the reminder of the fire we started?
The flame that humankind willed into existence in desperation.
Or is it fear?
The remnants of something we need to survive,
but could die in the thrashing embrace of.
Does it arouse us,
to watch the smoke?
The lingering aftermath of the thing that we feign control of,
But are at the mercy of?
Do we envy the smoke?
(If I could disappear as quickly as I appeared,
I would.)
In my 65-degree bedroom,
On a duvet covered in dog fur,
She puts her cigarette out by smashing it between two fingers.
Like a final period placed on a hand-penned letter.
I reach out to touch her,

But she rolls over and her mind escapes
to an empty corner of the ceiling.
Knee-deep into my own cliché,
I sink.

ABSENCE MAKES THE HEART GROW FONDER

When he is away from me,
my heart reaches from my chest like a wet toddler in a crib.
His voice fills my ears like brown whiskey in a crystal glass,
occupying every single tessellate crevice.
When he is away, his smile shines like sun on fresh snow,
And his eyes flicker like chunks of glitter
falling through the clear goo in a snow globe.
When he is away,
His touch seems hot and scarlet red.
Feverish and desirable.

When he is with me,
My heart retreats like a salty oyster into its shell.
His voice rips through me like a scissor in a seam.
When he is with me,
his smile is so loud I hear it with my eyes shut
And his nose drips
and his mouth drools
and his hands are clammy and awkward.

He is gilded in light from 5 feet away.
He is bothersome from 3.
Why can I love him,
only when he leaves?

READY

I knew I was ready to forgive you
When I wrenched the knife from my back
I held it up high
and it cast a menacing shadow
over the face of the young man in front of me.
Its shiny metal gleamed and glistened.
I stood heaving
and the veins in my face erupted
like tree branches gnarled into the forest floor.
I held the weapon
retrieved from my own back.
I gripped it once,
twice,
and then

I put it down.

REFRIGERATOR BLUE

2 eyes
the cold comfortable blue
of a refrigerator light
glowing in the temptation of a midnight snack.
How I rub your head
with my fingertips
and press my open palm against your skull
like I could push right through the bone
and grab a gushy handful of your brain
and take a chunk of it home with me
to devour later.
In my underwear,
off a plate,
in that refrigerator light,
like cold Chinese.
Grip my face
and scold me
for taking more than you wanted to give,
and I can feel my smile rising
push my cheeks through your fingers
like a handful of clay,
malleable in your grasp.
I'll miss your lap
and the heat between my legs
and showering off my sticky thighs
in the quiet when I get home.
Oh will I miss the stern, saccharine voice
melting from your lips
hovering over my open hungry mouth.

THE CAVE

I don't suppose I really know you very well—
but I know you smell like the delicious damp grass
that grows near old walls
and that your hands
are beautiful
opening out of your sleeves
and that the back of your head
is a mossy sheltered cave
when there is trouble in the wind
and that my cheek
just fits
the depression in your shoulder
and that is all I need to know.

PARASITE

I thought I knew what a muse was until I met him.
I'd been inspired before.
I'd been intrigued.
But I had no idea what a muse was
until he put his pink lips to my neck
and spit parasites into my ears.

Let them climb in and make a home
in the soft tissue of my brain.
Bred
and multiplied
and bit into my mind
till the memories of him opened
like sores
and festered in the heat of my anxiety.

I opened my mouth
and Times New Roman print flew out
like a plague of moths from its depths.

For 48 hours I was held captive
by the college-ruled lines
of a composition notebook.
Wrapped around my wrists
like the leather-bound work of a dominatrix.
He cracked a whip against my skin
and sliced my flesh open,
scarlet
like the margin taunting me.
The violet bruises on my neck,
my chest,
could hardly compare to the scar
that rose when he petrified me.
He shocked me.
Terrified me.
Because he inspired me.
I wasn't prepared
for the chaos that would follow.
A muse.
A parasite.
A symbiotic relationship.
Feed his hungry mind from my open mouth.

FOREVER CURSED IN LOVE ARE THE OBSERVANT

My mouth tastes like cinnamon whiskey
and menthol cigarettes.
Cabernet Sauvignon,
spearmint gum
and your hot heavy breath.
My mouth tastes like all the things
I should have said.
I don't want to be this way,
but I have been since you left.
I should have never counted your eyelashes
when you slept.
I should forget the way you take your tea,
but it haunts me.
2 sugars,
please.

THE PATTERN

What will be left
when I have broken all of my favorite things?
When the glue of sweet apologies
and bat eyelashes no longer repairs them?
What will be left when I have shattered it all?
Carelessly, it will evade my grasp.
And I will have
nothing.

I WOULD LEAVE ME IF I COULD.

This must be a nightmare.
It couldn't be a dream.
I'm washing in the shower,
my limbs clean,
until they bleed.
I sometimes miss the quiet;
the chaos of the streets.
I keep it all inside my mind
and every night
I scream.

I can't remember
what it's like to smell the ocean.
I can't remember
what it's like to feel the sea.
I can't remember what it's like to face a mirror
and not hate the person staring back at me.

I wish that I were dead
or at least somewhere else.
I try to keep the riot quiet
like a diet
for my health.

Stealth.
It's moving silently.
It's heavy.
It started from my knees
and now it's creeping up already.
Just another second now,
'cause here comes the confetti.
Please, hold the camera steady.

I encore 7 more
and everybody's like "That's plenty!"

I would leave me if you'd let me
I would leave me if you'd let me
I would leave me if I could.

BRIGHT EYES

They told me that she's beautiful
with bright eyes and fair skin.
She's from a city off the coast somewhere
where the girls are "made for men."
Is she a naked mess in underwear
on a dirty bathroom floor?
Do you look at her disgusted,
thinking that you deserve more?

But does she scream at the top of her lungs
praying you don't leave her?
Does she scream from an open mouth
begging you to feed her?

Will she set alarms obsessively
to check in on your breath?
Does she know the ways to touch you
with her lips upon your neck?
Is she agreeable and careless?
Does she answer all your calls?
Because I know you needed someone
who was fine with feeling small.

But does she scream at the top of her lungs
praying that you'll need her?
Do you scream at the top of your lungs?
Do your veins bleed her?

DEVIL IN ME

I won't take anyone down
If I crawl tonight
But I still let everyone down
When I change in size
And I went tumbling down
Trying to reach your height
But I scream too loud
If I speak my mind.

BRING ON THE BLACK!

Can't decide what's fake and what's fact
So you're up late screaming, "Bring on the black!"
Smoked so many cigarettes alone on a bathroom sink
I think my lungs are full to the brim with ink
And I can't get it past my throat to my fingers
to the paper
to the stingers
of the hive in my head
Last week I had a dream you were dead
I was on the phone calling
Begging for your body back
Screaming, "Bring on the black!"
I'm opening a faucet and I'm scared to let it run
It's been easier the past few months
when I would hold my tongue
'Cause when I write it all down I have to face it
But when I hold it inside I can pretend it's okay
I haven't called my grandmother in a year
'Cause she's the only one I know
Who tells me shit I don't wanna hear
But I need to hear
I've been in the gym these mornings
It takes me 7 minutes to run a mile
And 7 seconds to run from my problems
I'm working on my lung capacity
Fun capacity
Uptight bitch
Take a breath and relax,
it isn't so bad.

Keep drinking keep dancing
Keep hopeless romancing
They say that keys open doors
But you handed all your keys
To your friends and they dip 'em in a powder sack
Screaming, "Bring on the black!"
And every single second is like late-night TV
A Skinemax freebie
Watch the night sweats
drip down his back
Yelling, "Bring on the black!"
My father said,
"You'll never belong to a man till I'm dead"
So we just belong to a bag instead.
Winners don't lose, right?
Except sleep.
Counting sheep.
Relentless beep.
Of the hotel TV.
Too high to react.
So I'm up late begging,
"Lord, bring on the black."

SOMETHING FOR THEM

This is to remind you that you are a lover.
That you melt at a glance
at a touch.
That you are a baby.
You are soft and fragile
and you need someone to tell you
that everything is going to be okay.
That you are an idiot
and you are going to fuck up
1 million more times the rest of your life.
But this is to remind you
that you are a statue, gilded in marble,
and there is white lightning in your eyes.
Change shape.
Give in.

SEVENTEEN

It was cold for California
when my phone rang half past 3,
my little brother's on the other line.
He's shaking like a leaf.

At 17 years old, he lost his
best friend on a field.
There's no battle in our history book
compared to how he feels.

Alabaster faces,
all lined up, turning gray.
I watched my brother hold a casket
before his graduation day.

The boy's poor mother cried
with screams that echoed through the town.
Like a Siren on a shoreline,
begging God to let her drown.

So my brother crawled beside her
and he got beneath the sheet.
He let a woman hold him,
so that she could make believe.

She said, "Your arms are a bit smaller,
and your hair has got a wave,
but you smell just like my little boy.
You've almost got his face."

So he lay there on the couch
until the sky turned red and tan.
And in a full-grown woman's arms,
my little brother was a man.

I LEFT THE PARTY

I looked through the window and saw the lights flicker
like salt and pepper flakes across the Tokyo skyline.
I saw the amber glowing from the floor lamp in the corner,
warming the room with its thick embrace.
I saw the pink in my lips and the orange in my eyes
and the blush across my chest.
And I wondered how could I have not noticed
the ways in which you dulled my senses
and stole the color from the world right before my eyes.
Of all the wrongs you committed,
the worst was keeping me from the beauty
in anything
that wasn't
you.

I WISH THAT I WERE MANIC ALL THE TIME

Be patient with me
When my limbs become trees
And my roots become reeds
And the sounds from my mouth start making sense

My mind is messy but it's beautiful
like I'm in utero
I don't say it often,
but I'm proud of the woman that I turned out to be

You might think I'm crazy
Wild and young and free
But really I'm just:
careful
quiet
overthinking
analyzing like
It's logic
over loving
and emotion
brought me nothing
but disaster
so I hold my drink
and sit right in the corner
smiling.

Wish I were a wild child like I say I am
Wish I really meant it when I say
that I don't give a damn
Wish that I were *manic all the time*.
Think I like me better
when I'm all outside the lines.

But my colors bleed
And they bleed bright red.
I keep this pistol near my bed
Inside my mouth
so I can keep my tongue from tearing up my head.

ABOUT THE AUTHOR

HALSEY, born Ashley Nicolette Frangipane, is a Grammy-nominated singer-songwriter. She lives in Los Angeles, California.